BJ BookLinks®

:: Journey Into Literature ::

The Treasure of Pelican Cove

bju press®

Greenville, South Carolina

Pages marked "Reproducible" may be copied by the educator as needed, but not for commercial resale. No part of this publication may be reproduced for storage in a retrieval system or transmitted in any form or by any means—electronic, mechanical, recording, etc.—without the prior written permission of the publisher. Reproduction of these materials for an entire school or school system is strictly prohibited.

NOTE:
The fact that materials produced by other publishers are referred to in this volume does not constitute an endorsement by Bob Jones University Press of the content or theological position of materials produced by such publishers. The position of the Bob Jones University Press, and the University itself, is well known. Any references and ancillary materials are listed as an aid to the student or the teacher and in an attempt to maintain the accepted academic standards of the publishing industry.

BookLinks: Journey into Literature for *The Treasure of Pelican Cove*

Designed by Dan VanLeeuwen and Wendy Searles
Written by Eileen M. Berry
Project editor: Becky J. Smith

© 1998 Journey Books
Published by Bob Jones University Press
Greenville, South Carolina 29614

Printed in the United States of America
All rights reserved

ISBN 978-1-57924-201-5

15   14   13   12   11   10   9   8   7   6   5   4

BookLinks are individual units based on full-length, grade-level-appropriate books published by Journey Books, a division of Bob Jones University Press. They are intended to enhance and enrich the basic reading curriculum, not to replace it.

Contents

▶ A pocket folder printed with complete directions for enrichment activities.

▶ A teacher's guide with carefully planned lessons, enrichment activities, and blackline reproducibles.

Goal

To provide reading instruction and experience that broadens and deepens the ability of students to know, comprehend, analyze, synthesize, and evaluate what they read.

Strategies

▶ Focus on scriptural applications that help build character and discernment.

▶ Directly instruct specific reading strategies and higher-order thinking skills.

▶ Foster an appreciation for literature and the enjoyment of reading.

▶ Integrate reading with the other subject areas.

▶ Provide enrichment experiences such as games, songs, arts and crafts, cooking projects, science investigations, and creative writing.

As a part of group reading instruction in the classroom, *BookLinks* may be used with any of the following plans.

▶ The most able readers read two or three of the novels at appropriate points during the school year. The average readers read the one or two most suited to their abilities at appropriate points. The least able readers read only the least difficult of the novels toward the end of the school year.

▶ All groups read the same novel at different points in the school year with adjustments in pacing and teaching strategies for varying abilities.

▶ All groups read the least difficult novel at the end of the school year with appropriate adjustments.

As a part of home reading instruction, *BookLinks* may be used by the home educator in the following ways.

▶ To challenge the advanced reader.

▶ To enhance basic instruction for the average reader.

▶ To interest and motivate the struggling or reluctant reader.

Lesson Plans

Reproducibles

Answer Key

Lesson 1

Objectives

The student will
- Infer information from the cover of the book.
- Use pictures to comprehend the meanings of new words.
- Apply the scriptural principle of kindness in speech.
- Discern motives and responses of characters.
- Identify each character by his attitudes and actions.

Planning the Trip

Gather
- ❑ Pictures of roadways over large bodies of water.
- ❑ Pictures of tropical flowers and trees. (If possible, include crape myrtle, sea grape, and sea oats.)
- ❑ Pictures of southern homes with widow's walks. (Pictures may be found in books, magazines, old calendars, travel brochures, etc.)
- ❑ A business-sized envelope for each student.
- ❑ A Bible.
- ❑ A copy of *The Treasure of Pelican Cove* for each student.

Prepare
- ❑ A copy of Reproducibles—Lesson 1A and 1B for each student.
- ❑ A list of the following words on the chalkboard:
  causeway
  crape myrtle
  sea grape
  sea oats
  widow's walk

Packing Up

Introducing the Story
Discuss the following questions with the students.
- ▶ Have you ever stayed with a grandparent without your parents being there? What did you enjoy about the experience?
- ▶ Have you ever visited the ocean? What things did you find at the ocean that you couldn't have found at your own house?
- ▶ What can you discover about *The Treasure of Pelican Cove* from its front cover? (*title, author, a story about a boy and a dog, takes place near an ocean*)

Developing Word Meaning
Display the pictures, relating each one to the various words in the list on the chalkboard. Read the following sentences. Ask the students to supply the missing parts with words from the chalkboard.

We drove over the river on the _____. (*causeway*)

I tasted some purple fruit from a _____ shrub. (*sea grape*)

We admired the pretty pink blossoms on the _____ tree. (*crape myrtle*)

The _____ on the roof looked like a platform with a railing. (*widow's walk*)

Granny told us that the tall grass along the coastline was called _____. (*sea oats*)

Traveling Along

Setting the Purpose
Tell the students to look for answers to the following questions as they read.
- ▶ How many characters do you meet in this chapter? (Hint: One character is not a person.) (*6*)
- ▶ Which one is the main character? (*Jimmy*)

Reading and Thinking
Direct the students to read silently pages 1-9. Ask the following questions.
- ▶ *[interpretive]* What can you tell about Jimmy's personality from the opening scene in the airport? (*energetic, happy, likes to ask questions, likes dogs, does not like to obey his older brother and sister*)

  [interpretive] Why is Elizabeth Anne embarrassed? (*because Jimmy is attracting other people's attention with his excited, active behavior*)

  [appreciative] Have you ever been embarrassed by a younger brother or sister?

Choose a student to read aloud the sentence on page 2 that describes how Elizabeth Anne looks when she is embarrassed.

- ▶ *[literal]* What is the name of the house where Granny lives? (*Land's End*)

  [critical] Why do you think the house is called Land's End? (*Accept any answer, but suggest that the house is so named because it is right beside the sea—where the land ends and the sea begins.*)

[interpretive] What does the author mean when she says that Granny's eyes misted? *(They began to fill with tears.)*

[interpretive] Why do Granny's eyes mist when she looks at Elizabeth Anne? *(because she looks so much like her mother did at that age)*

[interpretive] Why do you think Paul elbows Jimmy when he starts to make a comment about how Elizabeth Anne looks? *(Answers might include that Paul doesn't think Jimmy should say something funny at a serious moment or that Jimmy might hurt his sister's feelings by commenting on her looks.)*

▶ *[interpretive]* How does Granny feel about Hiram? *(She often disagrees with him but considers him her good friend.)*

[interpretive] What do you think Granny means when she says, "Some things are better left unsaid"? *(She was probably going to say something critical about Hiram but decided against it.)*

Choose a student to read aloud the paragraph on pages 3 and 4 that tells what Granny thinks of Hiram's work.

▶ *[literal]* Where does Jimmy want to stop on the way to Granny's house? *(the amusement park)*

[interpretive] What does Granny think of the amusement park? *(She doesn't like it; she thinks it is there only for a tourist trap.)*

[critical] What do you think a *tourist trap* is? *(possible answer: a way to draw more tourists to the island)*

[appreciative] Would you have liked to stop at the amusement park?

▶ *[interpretive]* Why does Granny step on the gas after she turns into the driveway? *(She wants to tease Hiram by startling him.)*

[interpretive] Who got the last laugh after all? Why? *(Hiram, because he pretended that he couldn't hear Granny's scolding.)*

[interpretive] How do the children feel about Hiram? *(They like him; they are glad to see him.)*

[literal] What exciting thing does Jimmy see when he looks out his bedroom window? *(Blackie is on the beach path with Hiram.)*

Choose a student to read aloud the paragraph on page 9 that tells what Jimmy does after he sees Blackie.

Scriptural Application

Ask the students to think, without responding orally, of someone with whom they often have trouble getting along. Remind them of the biblical command to show kindness in our words always (Eph. 4:29, 32; Prov. 31:26).

Pausing to Rest

Tell the students that this leg of the journey is over, but many more adventures lie ahead. Direct them to mark their places in their books.

Going Further

Journey with the Author
Share the information in the author profile on the folder.

Journey into Thinking Skills—Convergent Thinking
See "What's the Treasure?" on the folder.

Journey into Story Elements—Characterization
"Who Is It?"
(Reproducible—Lesson 1A)

Journey into Vocabulary
"What's to See at the Sea?"
(Reproducible—Lesson 1B) See Teacher's Guide on the reverse side.

Journey into Information—Oceans and Shore Life
Place in the classroom reading center books about plant and animal life in and around the ocean.

Chapter 2, pages 11-19
Lesson 2

Objectives

The student will

- Understand that people have different values and tastes.
- Use context clues to comprehend the meanings of new words.
- Apply the scriptural principle of laying up treasure in heaven.
- Identify true and false statements about the story.

Planning the Trip

Gather

- ❑ A decorative box of any size.
- ❑ Materials to use with "A Sea Scene," as described on the folder.
- ❑ A Bible.

Prepare

- ❑ A copy of Reproducibles—Lesson 2A and 2B for each student.
- ❑ A list of the following words on the chalkboard:
  crestfallen
  whitecaps
  hurricane lamps

Packing Up

Introducing the Story

Show the students the box you have brought. Tell them that it is a box to hold treasures. Ask them what is meant by the word *treasure*. *(something valuable or precious)*

Direct the students to close their eyes and imagine that they have a box like this but with room enough inside to hold anything they want to put in it. Ask the following questions.

► What kinds of things are "treasures" to you? What would you keep in this box?

► Are those same things treasures to your brother or sister? What different things might he or she keep in the box?

Developing Word Meaning

Read each of the following sentences and choose students to tell which word from the chalkboard would best fit each blank.

The wind rose, and _____ rolled onto the beach from the sea. *(whitecaps)*

Anyone who looked at Jimmy's drooping mouth could tell he was _____. *(crestfallen)*

The candle flames flickered inside the glass of the _____. *(hurricane lamps)*

Traveling Along

Setting the Purpose

Tell the students that in this chapter, a treasure will be discovered. Encourage them to watch for this discovery as they read.

Reading and Thinking

Direct the students to read silently pages 11-19. Ask the following questions.

► [interpretive] Why is Jimmy sad when Hiram says he hasn't changed? *(He wishes he looked older as Elizabeth Anne and Paul do.)*

[literal] What advice does Hiram give Jimmy? *(Don't be in such a hurry to grow up.)*

[appreciative] Would you be interested in hearing a story about a pirate named Old Black Jack?

[literal] What kept Hiram from telling his story that night? *(A storm came, and he was busy tying things down so that they wouldn't blow away.)*

[interpretive] What changes in the scenery warn about the coming storm? *(sky turning gray, whitecaps racing to land, pelicans huddling on the rocks)*

Choose a student to read aloud the paragraph on page 13 that tells about these changes of scenery.

► [interpretive] Why did Granny gather flashlights and candles and hurricane lamps for the storm? *(to use if the electricity went out)*

[literal] Did Granny's preparations turn out to be useful? *(Yes, the lights went out.)*

[interpretive] How can you tell that Granny is a little nervous about letting Jimmy go out on the widow's walk in an approaching storm? *(She hesitates when he asks her; she tells him they can't stay up very long once they get there; she warns him not to lean over the edge.)*

[critical] Why would a widow's walk not be a very safe place during a storm? *(Accept any answer, but lead the students to understand that high winds might be able to break rails or blow a small boy over the edge.)*

[literal] Where does Granny think Blackie has gone? *(to the amusement park to chase squirrels)*

[literal] Who makes sure he gets safely home? *(Hiram)*

Choose a student to read aloud the paragraph at the bottom of page 14 and the top of page 15 that tells what Jimmy and Granny see from the widow's walk.

▶ *[literal]* What does Jimmy say he learns from Granny every summer? *(character)*

[interpretive] What do you think he means by character? *(Answers might include learning how to do right or learning how to obey the Bible.)*

[literal] What do the children go to the beach to do the morning after the storm? *(look for things that the storm has washed ashore)*

[appreciative] Have you ever hunted for shells on a beach?

[literal] What does Jimmy want to find? *(a big shell like Hiram's)*

[literal] What special treasure does Jimmy find at the end of the chapter, and where does he find it? *(a green jewel wrapped in a ball of clay that Blackie brings to him)*

Choose a student to read aloud the paragraph on page 17 that describes the treasures Jimmy and Hiram find on the beach after the storm.

Scriptural Application

Read Matthew 6:19-20. Ask the students where the Lord tells us to lay up our treasures. *(heaven)* Direct a discussion about what Jesus meant when He said to lay up treasure in heaven. *(spending our time, money, and energy on things that will count for eternity—praying for others, witnessing, learning to love God more, etc.)*

Pausing to Rest

Tell the students that in the next chapter the children will learn the story behind the treasure. Direct them to mark their places in their books.

Going Further

Journey into Comprehension
"X or O?"
(Reproducible—Lesson 2A)

Journey into Arts and Crafts
Direct the students in making a sea scene as described on the folder. (Use Reproducible—Lesson 2B as needed.) You may wish to keep the students' projects on display for a further activity in Lesson 5.

Journey into Language— Speaking
Encourage the students to bring in "treasures" they have found while visiting the sea and "show-and-tell" about them to the class.

Journey into Information— Hurricanes
Provide library books or a science video about hurricanes. Conduct a discussion about what people do to prepare for hurricanes.

Lesson3

Objectives

The student will

- Recognize elements of a good story.
- Use context clues to comprehend the meanings of new words.
- Apply the scriptural principle of speaking truthfully.
- Recall facts and details from the story.

Planning the Trip

Gather

- ❏ Lemonade.
- ❏ A paper cup for each student.
- ❏ A piece of clothing or a picture with embroidery on it.
- ❏ A Bible.

Prepare

- ❏ A copy of Reproducible—Lesson 3A for each student.
- ❏ Reproducible—Lesson 3B as noted on the reverse side.
- ❏ A list of the following words on the chalkboard:
  - piece of eight
  - indignantly
  - embroider
  - cache

Packing Up

Introducing the Story

Give each student a cup of lemonade to drink while you direct the following discussion.

▶ What kinds of stories do you like to have read or told to you? Direct a brief discussion about what makes a story exciting and fun to listen to. You might discuss such things as interesting characters, suspense, facial and vocal expression of the storyteller, and so on.

Explain that Chapter 3 of *The Treasure of Pelican Cove* contains a "story within a story." In the story, the children listen to another story—and the reader gets to "listen in" too.

Developing Word Meaning

Read the phrase *piece of eight* from the chalkboard.

> This was a name for a Spanish coin called a peso during the reign of King Charles III of Spain. It got its name because it was worth eight reals and had the numeral *8* stamped on it. It was valued at 12½¢.

Read the word *indignantly* from the chalkboard. Ask the students what they think it means in this sentence.

> When Richard told the teacher I had cheated, I said indignantly, "I did not!" *(angrily)*

Read the word *embroider* from the chalkboard. Tell the students that some words can have either a good or a bad meaning, depending on how they are used. Show the students the piece of embroidery you have brought and then read the following sentence.

> Sometimes people embroider on a plain piece of fabric to make it fancier or prettier.

After giving the students a chance to guess the meaning of the word *embroider*, lead them to understand that it means "to add decorative details." Point out that *embroider* has a good meaning when used in this way. Now read the following sentence.

> Because she likes to embroider the truth, people never know whether to believe her.

▶ Does *embroider* have a good or bad meaning in this sentence? What does it mean? *(bad—to stretch the truth, lie, exaggerate)*

Read the word *cache* from the chalkboard.

▶ What word does it sound like? *(cash, meaning "money")*

Ask them what they think the word means in this sentence.

> The squirrel had a large cache for its nuts. *(hiding place)*

Traveling Along

Setting the Purpose

Tell the students to watch for the place where the "story within a story" begins as they read this chapter.

Reading and Thinking

Direct the students to read silently pages 21-27. Ask the following questions.

▶ *[literal]* Why do Granny, Hiram, and the children rush out to meet Jimmy when he comes up from the beach? *(He is running and shouting with excitement; they are afraid he is hurt.)*

[interpretive] Why does Granny frown at Hiram and speak sternly to him? *(She is afraid he is making up the story about Pegleg.)*

[interpretive] What does Hiram mean when he says he "embroiders" stories sometimes? *(He adds to them to make them more exciting.)*

[critical] Why does Granny want Hiram to warn them when he is telling a "needlework story"? *(It would be wrong for him to claim that a story he has "spiced up" is the truth.)*

[critical] Is it wrong to make up stories? *(No, point out that it is wrong only to make them up for the purpose of deceiving someone.)*

[critical] What makes Hiram's story a good one? *(Accept any answer, but point out that Hiram uses descriptive language at the beginning to set a mood for the story, and he withholds important information until the end to create suspense.)*

[appreciative] Do you know someone who is good at storytelling? Choose a student to read aloud Granny's parting words to Hiram on page 23 when she leaves to get the lemonade.

▶ *[literal]* How did Hiram's granddad know the pirate had a peg leg? *(The tracks in the sand were one foot, one circle.)*

[interpretive] What is a peg leg? *(an artificial wooden leg)*

[critical] Why do you think Granny disapproved of Granddad's continuing to search for the treasure? *(possible answer: because he wasted time wandering the beach and was greedy)*

[literal] How does Hiram know Pegleg's treasure has to be close by? *(because Pegleg had to bury it while his granddad was unconscious, which was only a few hours)*

Choose a student to read aloud the paragraph on page 27 that describes a common method of burying treasure.

Scriptural Application

Read Ephesians 4:25. Ask the students what it means to "put away lying." *(stop telling lies)* Remind them that once we are saved, God wants us to stop telling lies and to speak the truth to one another.

Pausing to Rest

Tell the students that they will soon find out what happens when others learn about Jimmy's discovery. Direct them to mark their places in their books.

Going Further

Journey into Information—Story Details
"A Chest of Missing Words" (Reproducible—Lesson 3A)

Journey into Science
"Whose Tracks?" (Reproducible—3B) See Teacher's Guide on the reverse side.

Journey into Language—Writing
Challenge the students to make up a pirate tale of their own and either write it down or tell it to a family member.

Chapter 4, pages 29-38
Lesson 4

Objectives

The student will

- Appreciate the uniqueness and variety of God's creation in the sea.
- Use context clues to comprehend the meanings of new words.
- Apply the scriptural principle of thanking God for making him unique and having a special purpose for him.
- Recognize elements of the story's setting found on an imaginary map of Pelican Cove.

Planning the Trip

Gather

❏ Pictures, live specimens, or shells of the following types of marine life: hermit crab, sea anemone, coral, angelfish, sunfish, snail.
❏ A Bible.

Prepare

❏ A copy of Reproducible—Lesson 4 for each student.
❏ A list of the following words on the chalkboard:
dunes
quadrants

Packing Up

Introducing the Story

Show the students the pictures, live specimens, and/or shells you have brought. Guide them in a discussion about the unique characteristics of each creature and the variety of God's creation in the sea.
Tell the students that each of these creatures will be mentioned in their reading for today.

Developing Word Meaning

Read the following sentences. Ask the students to supply the missing parts with words from the chalkboard.

The wind had blown the sand into little hills called _____. *(dunes)*

Our guide sectioned the map into four parts, or four _____. *(quadrants)*

Traveling Along

Setting the Purpose

Tell the students to note the references to the sea creatures they have learned about as they read.

Reading and Thinking

Direct the students to read silently pages 29-38. Ask the following questions.

▶ *[interpretive]* Why does Granny disapprove of the children's desire to dig for treasure? *(She thinks it is a waste of time since there is nothing there for them to find.)*

[literal] What disease does Granny say the children have? *(treasure-hunting fever)*

[interpretive] What does she mean by calling it a fever? *(It causes excitement, makes people act crazy, but doesn't last.)*

[critical] Granny tells Hiram she is holding him responsible for the children. What does she mean by that? *(Accept any answer, but lead the students to the conclusion that she is trusting Hiram to take care of them and keep them from getting hurt.)*

Choose a student to read aloud the paragraphs on page 30 that tell about Granny's warning and Hiram's response.

▶ *[literal]* What do the children argue about at the beginning of the search? *(They all want to start searching in different spots.)*

[literal] How does Blackie give them a new idea? *(He runs ahead to follow his regular route; they realize the jewels are hidden somewhere in his territory since he must have found the jewel along his route.)*

[literal] What plan do Hiram and Paul come up with? *(to draw a map of Blackie's territory and search it in quadrants)*

[interpretive] What thing in Hiram's apartment does Jimmy seem most interested in? *(the fish tank)*

[appreciative] Which creature in the tank would have interested you the most?

Choose a student to read aloud the paragraph on page 35 that describes the huge saltwater tank.

▶ *[interpretive]* What problem does Paul have as he tries to dig in the sand? *(Water keeps filling the hole up again.)*

[critical] Do you think it would be wise to somehow mark the spot if you were planning to bury a treasure? *(Accept any answer, but lead the students to understand that it would.)*

[interpretive] Why does Hiram think Granny might be able to help? *(because she has lived here all her life and will know about any changes)*

[literal] What surprise is waiting for Hiram and the children when they reach the house? *(Granny and the emerald are gone.)*

Choose a student to read the sentence on page 38 that tells which two things are missing from Land's End.

Scriptural Application

Read Psalm 139:14 to the students. Explain that just as God designed each sea creature with its own unique characteristics, He has also made each one of us in a unique way. Remind them that when we have something about ourselves that is different from others, whether a physical difference or a difference in ability or skill, we should thank God for making us unique and for having a special purpose for each individual He has created.

Pausing to Rest

Tell the students that they will have to wait to find out what has become of Granny. Direct them to mark their places in their books.

Going Further

Journey into Heritage Studies—Maps

"*X* Marks the Spot" (Reproducible—Lesson 4) Keep for use in Lesson 9.

Journey into Science

Direct the students in the investigation of seawater, as noted on the folder.

Journey into Art

Allow the students to draw pictures showing how they think Hiram's aquarium might have looked. Make the pictures of the sea creatures available for them to refer to as they draw.

Lesson 5

Objectives

The student will

- Understand the importance of discernment in speech.
- Use context clues to comprehend the meanings of new words.
- Apply the scriptural principle of refusing to be a talebearer.

Planning the Trip

Gather

❏ The students' projects for "A Sea Scene" from Lesson 2.
❏ A Bible.

Prepare

❏ A copy of Reproducibles—Lesson 5A and 5B for each student.
❏ A list of the following definitions on the chalkboard:
   someone who oversees a museum
   someone who is nosy
   people who watch
   muscular
   moved about to inspect or keep order
❏ A word card for each of the following words:
   curator
   busybody
   onlookers
   beefy
   patrolled

Packing Up

Introducing the Story

Play the game "telephone," demonstrating how information can change as it travels from person to person.

Seat the students in a circle.

Whisper in the ear of one of the students the sentence "Sarah feeds fish to six white kittens."

Direct that student to whisper the sentence he heard to the person on his left and so on around the circle.

Direct the last student in the circle to tell the class the sentence he heard.

If the sentence is unchanged, try playing the game again with a different sentence. If the sentence has changed, ask the students why they think it changed. (*Accept any answer, but point out that it is often hard to repeat something exactly as you heard it.*)

Explain to the students that this game is a good example of how rumors can get started when news travels through many different people. Remind the students of the importance of telling *only* the truth and knowing when even the truth is meant to be kept secret. Tell them that in today's reading they will learn about some rumors that got started in Pelican Cove.

Developing Word Meaning

Read the definitions on the chalkboard to the students. Read the following sentences, displaying the word cards for the italicized words. After each sentence, choose a student to match a definition from the list with the card.

Old *busybody* Culpepper is not known for keeping secrets. (*someone who is nosy*)

If you have any questions about the museum displays, ask the *curator*. (*someone who oversees a museum*)

That weightlifter is a *beefy* man. (*muscular*)

The firemen told the *onlookers* to go home. (*people who watch*)

A policeman *patrolled* the area where the criminal had escaped. (*moved about to inspect or keep order*)

Traveling Along

Setting the Purpose

Encourage the students to notice some of the rumors the people in Pelican Cove have heard about the treasure.

Reading and Thinking

Direct the students to read silently pages 39-48. Ask the following questions.

▶ *[interpretive]* How do you think Hiram and the children are feeling while they wait for Granny to return? (*nervous, excited, perhaps worried that something bad has happened to her*)

[literal] Where has Granny been? (*to the museum to talk to Mr. Culpepper about the emerald*)

[literal] What good news does Granny bring? (*There is a finder's fee for the emerald.*)

[critical] Why do Granny and Hiram think so many people will want to help search for the treasure? (*Accept any answer, but point*

out that most people will want to find treasure so that they can get a finder's fee too.)

[appreciative] What would you do with the money if you won the finder's fee?

Choose a student to read aloud the paragraph on page 41 that explains why the children will have so many helpers on their treasure hunt.

▶ *[interpretive]* How do the children feel after their first day of treasure hunting? *(tired, hungry)*

[literal] What does Jimmy see out the window early the next morning? *(holes on the beach, people hunting for treasure)*

[interpretive] What does Miss Abbott start to say but does not finish? *(For years everyone had thought Hiram's grandfather was crazy to keep searching for the treasure.)*

[interpretive] What figure of speech doesn't Jimmy understand? *(lost his marbles)*

[interpretive] How do you know Jimmy doesn't understand its meaning? *(He says they didn't find any marbles.)*

[interpretive] What does Hiram think of the man with the bulldozer? *(He is angry with him; he doesn't want him to use the bulldozer.)*

Choose a student to read aloud the paragraph on page 44 that tells of Hiram's response to the man driving the bulldozer.

▶ *[critical]* Where do you think the crowd has gotten its strange ideas about how much treasure has been found? *(Accept all answers, but lead the students to realize that someone started a rumor and others added to the story until it was far from the truth.)*

[interpretive] Why is the volunteer police department needed to patrol the beach? *(to make sure no one comes and tries to dig for treasure)*

[interpretive] Why do you think Jake refuses to leave? *(Answers may vary but might include that he wants to make sure no one else gets to the treasure before he does or perhaps that he wants to help keep watch on the beach.)*

[literal] What does Jimmy decide about Jake? *(to keep out of his way)*

[critical] What kind of person do you think Jake is? *(Accept any answer.)*

Choose a student to read aloud the last two paragraphs on page 48 in which Jimmy and Blackie decide to avoid Jake.

Scriptural Application

Read Proverbs 11:13 to the students. Ask them what they think a talebearer is. *(one who spreads rumors or tells lies)* Ask the students what they should do when they are tempted to tell someone something that they are not sure is true or that was meant to be a secret. *(Accept all answers, but lead them to understand that they should pray for the Lord's help and then keep quiet or try to talk about something else instead.)*

Pausing to Rest

Ask the students whether they think Jake might show up again in this story. *(Accept any answer.)* Direct them to mark their places in their books.

Going Further

Journey into Thinking Skills—Comprehension
"Filling in the Holes"
(Reproducible—Lesson 5A)

Journey into Language—Writing
"What If?"
(Reproducible—Lesson 5B)

Journey into Heritage Studies
In a reading center, provide library books about the California Gold Rush of 1849, a case of "treasure fever" in American history.

Chapter 6, pages 49-56
Lesson 6

Objectives

The students will

- Recognize character motivation.
- Use context clues to comprehend the meanings of new words.
- Apply the scriptural principle of being a peacemaker.
- Recall the sequence of events in the story.

Planning the Trip

Gather

- ❑ Pictures of jewels and precious stones from magazine advertisements or catalogs, showing prices of each.
- ❑ Materials to use with "Shadows," as described on the folder.
- ❑ A Bible.

Prepare

- ❑ A copy of Reproducible—Lesson 6 for each student.
- ❑ A list of the following sentences on the chalkboard:

  I probed under my bed, searching for my baseball cap.

  The crab scuttled away before I could catch it.

  "Stop!" I shouted furiously to the thief.

  The house's dark, silent windows showed that it had been vacated long ago.

  The pier jutted out from the beach.

Packing Up

Introducing the Story

Allow the students to pass the pictures of jewels around the classroom. Ask them which type of jewel they would like to find if they were digging for treasure in Pelican Cove. Direct their attention to the prices they see on the pages.

Discuss the following questions with the students.

▶ Why do you think the prices are so high? (*Accept any answer, but lead the students to understand that jewels are high priced because they are beautiful and rare.*)

▶ Why are the people in the town of Pelican Cove so eager to find more jewels? (*They want the riches and recognition that finding jewels would bring them.*)

▶ Is it wrong to have jewelry and nice things? (*Lead them to see that it is not, but it is wrong to place more importance on those things than on things that God values.*)

Discuss what types of things God values.

Developing Word Meaning

Read the sentences on the chalkboard. Then read each question, directing the students to choose one of the underlined words from the list on the chalkboard for their answer.

Which word means "angrily or fiercely"? (*furiously*)

Which word means "ran with swift, hurried movements"? (*scuttled*)

Which word means "extended outward"? (*jutted*)

Which word means "left empty"? (*vacated*)

Which word means "explored"? (*probed*)

Traveling Along

Setting the Purpose

Tell the students to look for reasons for the title "Dark Shadows" as they read this chapter.

Reading and Thinking

Direct the students to read silently pages 49-56. Ask the following questions.

▶ [literal] Why does Jimmy think that he can't go out to play with Blackie? (*because the beach is off-limits*)

[literal] What new information does Granny give Jimmy? (*The beach is closed only for digging, not for regular use.*)

[interpretive] How can you tell Jimmy was excited about going out to play on the beach with Blackie? (*He didn't wait for Granny to finish; he half-ran, half-slid down the path to get to the beach quickly.*)

[literal] What does Jimmy find in the hole on the beach? (*a starfish*)

[appreciative] Have you ever touched a starfish? What did it feel like?

Choose a student to read aloud the paragraph on page 51 where Jimmy plays with the starfish.

▶ [literal] What frightens Jimmy? (*A shadow falls across a dune and Blackie barks furiously, but no one answers when Jimmy calls.*)

[literal] What does Jimmy tell Granny back at the house? *(that someone had been watching him)*

[interpretive] Why does Elizabeth Anne think treasure hunting isn't fun anymore? *(Answers may include that too many people are searching for the treasure; the other people cannot be trusted; it has become dangerous to be alone on the beach.)*

[critical] What do you think would have to happen for everything to be "back the way it used to be"? *(Answers will vary; emphasize that people would have to stop being greedy for the jewels.)*

Choose a student to read aloud what Granny tells Elizabeth Anne on page 53.

▶ *[literal]* What happens at the town meeting? *(People argue and make long speeches; they decide to divide the beach up into sections and allow only hand-digging.)*

[interpretive] How does Granny feel about the decision? *(angry, disappointed in the people of her town for being so greedy)*

[critical] Why do you think Granny reads the story about Rachel's idols from the Bible? *(Answers will vary; point out that Rachel's greed in taking the idols caused an argument between Jacob and Laban. Granny was probably trying to make a point about how greed can drive people to fight and argue.)*

Choose two students to read aloud on page 53 the responses of Hiram and Jimmy to the meeting.

▶ *[literal]* What do Granny and Hiram find funny about the people digging on the beach? *(Some are working harder than they have ever been known to work before; they are all getting good exercise if nothing else.)*

[literal] What happens to anger Jimmy? *(One of Jake's workers chases Blackie with a shovel.)*

[literal] Why does Jake offer to buy Blackie? *(He thinks Blackie can lead him right to the treasure.)*

[critical] Why do you think this chapter is called "Dark Shadows"? *(Accept any answer. Possible meanings of "shadows" include the following: the shadow Jimmy sees on the beach, the "bitter taste" that has come of Granddad's treasure because of all the arguing, Jimmy's feeling frightened by Jake and his workers.)*

Choose a student to read aloud Jimmy's response to Jake on page 56 when he offers Jimmy money for his dog.

Scriptural Application

Ask the students what God thinks of arguing and quarreling. *(He is not pleased with it.)* Read Matthew 5:9, Romans 12:18, and Philippians 2:14. Ask them to name ways they could help make peace when a quarrel is about to begin over which game to play on the playground. *(Answers may include keeping calm, listening to the other person's idea, being willing to try new things, not insisting on their own way, suggesting they play one game for half the recess time and then the other game.)*

Pausing to Rest

Tell the students that after Jimmy's experience with Jake, he probably needs some time to calm down. Direct them to mark their places in their books.

Going Further

Journey into Thinking Skills—Sorting and Ordering
"Arranging Shells"
(Reproducible—Lesson 6)

Journey into Science
Read the information on the folder about shadows to the students and direct the shadow-drawing activity.

Lesson 7

Objectives

The student will

- Relate personal experiences to story content.
- Use context clues to comprehend the meanings of new words.
- Apply the scriptural principle of prayer and trust.
- Create a story of his own that relates to chapter content.

Planning the Trip

Gather

❏ A Bible.

Prepare

❏ A transparency of Reproducible—7A.
❏ A copy of Reproducible—Lesson 7B for each student.
❏ A list of the following sentences on the chalkboard:

The detective put a <u>bug</u> on the suspect's phone in order to hear his conversations.

The police had the house under <u>surveillance</u>, waiting for the robber to come out.

I wonder if the store would <u>refund</u> the money I spent for this shirt.

The car <u>merged</u> with the other cars that were speeding down the busy highway.

Packing Up

Introducing the Story

Discuss the following questions with the students.

▶ Have you ever lost something important?

▶ What methods did you use to try to find the lost object?

▶ Where did you finally find it?

Explain that in today's reading something important is lost, and Hiram and the children find some helpful clues.

Developing Word Meaning

Read the sentences from the chalkboard. Ask the following questions.

Which word means "close watch"? *(surveillance)*

Which word means "blended together"? *(merged)*

Which word means "pay back"? *(refund)*

Which word means "an electronic listening device"? *(bug)*

Traveling Along

Setting the Purpose

Encourage the students to notice what important thing is lost and who finds the helpful clues.

Reading and Thinking

Direct the students to read silently pages 57-64. Ask the following questions.

▶ *[interpretive]* Why do you think Jimmy wants Blackie to sleep in the house? *(so no one can steal him during the night)*

[literal] Why is Jimmy near tears in the morning? *(Blackie is gone, and he expects the worst.)*

[literal] How does Granny comfort him? *(She tells Jimmy that Blackie always gets up early in the morning, and she has let him out herself.)*

[literal] Why does Blackie chase squirrels? *(for exercise and because there are no cats around to chase)*

[interpretive] How does Jimmy feel about taking care of Blackie? *(He loves to do it; he looks on it as his own special job.)*

Choose a student to read aloud the paragraph on page 58 where Jimmy describes each child's responsibilities.

▶ *[interpretive]* Why does Hiram say that the diggers are wasting their time? *(because Blackie is the only one who really knows where to find the treasure)*

[literal] What does Hiram suggest for finding the treasure? *(putting a bug on Blackie and a listening bug on Jimmy)*

[interpretive] What does Granny mean when she says, "I have a responsibility to your parents"? *(The children's parents are trusting her to take care of them, and if they get hurt, she would be in trouble.)*

[critical] What does it mean to "feel responsible" for something or someone? *(possible answer: to feel as if it is your job to take care of them)*

[appreciative] What are you responsible for doing in your home?

Choose a student to read aloud Granny's response to Hiram on page 61 after he tells her he will stay with the children every step of the way.

▶ *[literal]* What offer does the salesman at the electronics store make? *(to let them rent the equipment for a week; if they return it in good condition, they'll get a refund)*

[literal] What bad news does Granny have for them when they return home? *(Blackie's gone.)*

[interpretive] Why does Jimmy immediately assume that Jake stole Blackie? *(because he had been so interested in buying him)*

[literal] What advice does Hiram give Jimmy? *(Settle down; wait to see if they find Blackie somewhere else.)*

[appreciative] Have you ever accused someone and then later found out you were wrong? How did you feel when this happened?

Choose a student to read aloud Granny's response to Jimmy on page 63 when he says that Jake got Blackie.

▶ *[literal]* What does Elizabeth Anne find that seems to prove Blackie has been stolen? *(boot tracks alongside the dog tracks, then no more tracks)*

[interpretive] How does Jimmy feel when he sees the tracks? *(sad, fearful that Blackie is in danger)*

Choose a student to read aloud Jimmy's response to his sister's discovery at the end of page 64.

Scriptural Application
Ask the students what advice they would give to Jimmy at this point. *(Accept any answer.)* Read Philippians 4:6 to the students. Ask them what this verse tells us to do in situations like Jimmy's. *(Do not worry but pray about your problem with thanksgiving.)* Tell the students this is not always an easy thing to do, but God promises to give us peace when we trust Him.

Pausing to Rest

Tell the students that they will have to wait until next time to find out where Blackie is. Direct them to mark their places in their books.

Going Further

Journey into Music
Sing the song "Where Has My Little Dog Gone?" with the students. (See Reproducible—Lesson 7A.)

Journey into Higher Order Reading Skills—Predicting Outcomes
"On the Right Track" (Reproducible—Lesson 7B)

Journey into Writing
Instruct the students to write a three- to five-sentence story about an important object that was lost and found again. The story may be true or fictional.

Lesson 8

Objectives

The student will

- Recognize the value of politeness.
- Use context clues to comprehend the meanings of new words.
- Apply the scriptural principle of getting all the facts before making a judgment.
- Infer character traits.

Planning the Trip

Gather

- ❏ A slice of banana-nut bread for each student.
- ❏ Butter.
- ❏ A paper plate and/or napkin for each student.
- ❏ A plastic knife for each student.
- ❏ A Bible.

Prepare

- ❏ A copy of Reproducible—Lesson 8A for each student.
- ❏ A list of the following words on the chalkboard:
  approach
  frenzy
  sullenly
  squatting
  precautions

Packing Up

Introducing the Story

Choose students to help you distribute plates, knives, and a slice of bread and butter to each person in the group.

Discuss the following questions with the students as they eat.

▶ What does it mean to be polite? *(being kind, considerate; using good manners)*

▶ What are some ways to be polite when visiting in a friend's home? *(Accept all answers.)*

▶ Why is politeness important? *(It shows others that we are thinking of them; it reflects well on the Lord when we are considerate of others.)*

Tell the students that in the chapter for today, Granny and the others will pay a neighborly visit to a Pelican Cove friend.

Developing Word Meaning

Tell the students that just as Jimmy is searching for a missing dog, you would like them to help you search for missing words. Tell them to pretend that they are like Blackie; they cannot talk but can only "bark."

Read the word list from the chalkboard. Read the following sentences. After each sentence, go down the list on the chalkboard, pointing to each word. Instruct the students to bark when you point to the word that best completes the sentence.

When you light a campfire, take _____ to keep the fire from getting out of control. *(precautions)*

A faraway whistle told us of the _____ of the train. *(approach)*

When the basketball went through the hoop at the sound of the buzzer, the crowd burst into a _____ of cheering. *(frenzy)*

He does not own the house; he is only _____ there for a few months. *(squatting)*

The girl who had been disrespectful sat _____ in the corner. *(sullenly)*

Ask a student to demonstrate a sullen face for the class.

Traveling Along

Setting the Purpose

Tell the students to pay close attention to how Granny treats her friend Mrs. Lester as they read this chapter. Encourage them to learn from her example of kindness.

Reading and Thinking

Direct the students to read silently pages 65-74. Ask the following questions.

▶ *[literal]* What does Granny suggest to help them get to the bottom of Blackie's disappearance? *(go to see Jake's ma)*

[interpretive] Why is Jimmy's face wet? *(He has been crying about Blackie.)*

[interpretive] Why didn't Jimmy want to look at the beach when they passed it? *(It would make him sad not to see Blackie there.)*

[appreciative] Have you ever lost something that you cared deeply about? How did you feel?

Choose a student to read aloud the paragraph on page 66 that describes how Jimmy acted during the trip to Mrs. Lester's house.

▶ [literal] What did the children expect Granny to ask Mrs. Lester about first? (Blackie) What did she ask about instead? (the weather)

[critical] Why do you think Granny asked other questions before getting to the real reason for the visit? (Possible answers: She was being polite; she didn't want Mrs. Lester to think she suspected her son of doing wrong.)

[literal] What comment makes Jimmy angry? (Mrs. Lester says that he looks like her Jake when things don't go his way.)

Choose a student to read aloud the paragraph on page 67 that lets you know Jimmy is angry.

▶ [literal] What does Granny ask Mrs. Lester when the subject comes around to Jake? (if he could help them find Blackie)

[interpretive] What did Jimmy want her to ask instead? (He thought she should ask if Jake had taken Blackie.)

Choose a student to read aloud Mrs. Lester's description of Jake on page 68.

▶ [literal] What happens to frighten Jimmy? (Jake comes home.)

[appreciative] Have you ever thought you knew what someone was like but have then seen a different side of the person?

[interpretive] What do you think Jake meant when he said, "It's not in my nature to hurt a dog"? (that he is not mean; that he loves dogs too much to hurt one)

Choose a student to read aloud the paragraph on page 69 that tells how Jake responds with compassion to Jimmy and his needs.

▶ [literal] Whose house does Jake take them to? (the stringy-haired man who chased Blackie)

[interpretive] What clue does the author give that Blackie might be at the stringy-haired man's house? (They hear barking when they pull into the driveway.)

Ask a student to demonstrate how someone might move when they are angry.

▶ [literal] How do the children react when they see Blackie? (They are very happy and excited; they run to him and pet him.)

[appreciative] How do you react when you find something that has been lost for a long time?

[interpretive] What does Jake mean when he says that "Bill's just squatting on this property"? (He does not own it.)

[interpretive] Why do you think Jimmy is a little embarrassed at the end of this chapter? (because he has accused someone wrongly)

[critical] Do you think Jimmy's opinion of Jake has changed at the end of the chapter? Why or why not? (Accept any answer.)

Choose a student to read Granny's advice in the paragraph at the bottom of page 73.

Scriptural Application

Read Proverbs 18:13 to the students. Ask them what this verse says about passing judgment on a person before knowing all the facts. (It is folly and shame.) Encourage the students to memorize this verse and obey it the next time they are tempted to accuse someone before they have proof of that person's guilt.

Pausing to Rest

Tell the students that Bill seems like someone they should keep an eye on in future chapters. Direct them to mark their places in their books.

Going Further

Journey into Story Elements— Characterization
"The 'Jake' Mistake"
(Reproducible—Lesson 8A)

Journey into Thinking Skills—Critical Thinking
"How Come?"
(Reproducible—Lesson 8B)

Lesson9

Objectives

The student will

- Recognize the importance of humor.
- Use textual clues to comprehend the meanings of new words.
- Apply the scriptural principle of accepting correction.

Planning the Trip

Gather

- ❏ A Bible.
- ❏ The students' finished copies of Repro-ducible—Lesson 4.

Prepare

- ❏ A copy of Reproducible—Lesson 9 for each student.
- ❏ A list of the following words on the chalkboard:
  securing
  kerosene
  dwindled
  breakwater

Packing Up

Introducing the Story

Ask the students whether they have ever read a story that made them laugh so hard they wanted to read it to someone else.
Discuss the following questions with the students.

▶ Why do we like to read funny things? *(they make us laugh or feel happy)*

▶ Why do we feel like sharing funny things with other people? *(to make them happy, to give them enjoyment)*

Explain that sometimes authors put funny parts into a story right after a serious, sad, or scary part. Ask the students why they think this is true. *(to let the reader relax again; to let him stop worrying for a while about what is going to happen)*

Developing Word Meaning

Read the list of words on the chalkboard and ask the following questions.

▶ Which word has a smaller word in it that means "safe"? *(securing)*
Tell the students that *securing* means "making something safe."

▶ Which word is made up of two smaller words? *(breakwater—* break *and* water*)*
Tell the students that a breakwater is a barrier that protects a shore from crashing waves; in other words, it "breaks" the force of the water before it hits the land.

▶ Of the two words left, which means "a thin oil used as fuel"? *(kerosene)*

▶ Which word means "became gradually less and less"? *(dwindled)*

Traveling Along

Setting the Purpose

Tell the students that they will find some humor in this chapter. Encourage them to notice which things make them laugh and to think about why the author put them in the book.

Reading and Thinking

Direct the students to read silently pages 75-83. Ask the following questions.

▶ *[interpretive]* Where does Granny finally pin Jimmy's bug? *(in his shirt pocket)*

[literal] What happens to make the family laugh when Jimmy starts out? *(He hunches his shoulder up to his head to try to talk into the bug.)*

[interpretive] What do you think Paul means when he says, "If he keeps this up, he'll be thrown off the beach"? *(People will see Jimmy's odd actions and think he is crazy.)*

[appreciative] Do you have a member of your family who makes you laugh sometimes?

[literal] What does Talmadge Duncan think Jimmy's problem is? *(chiggers)* What advice does he give him? *(to try kerosene)*

Choose two students to read aloud Jimmy and Talmadge's conversation at the top of page 77.

▶ [literal] What is Elizabeth Anne's job? (writing down Jimmy's comments)

[literal] What is Paul's job? (tracking Blackie's movements on a map)

[critical] Which do you think would be more difficult and why? (Accept any answer.)

[interpretive] Why does Hiram think it is important to keep track of all the information? (so that no clue will be overlooked)

Choose a student to read aloud on page 78 Hiram's reasoning for writing down everything Jimmy says.

▶ [literal] What does Jimmy do that makes the family nervous? (goes out onto the breakwater)

[critical] Do you think it was right for Jimmy to follow Blackie out onto the rocks? (Accept any answer, but lead the students to understand that it wasn't; Granny had already told him he couldn't play there.)

[interpretive] How can you tell that Granny was upset with Jimmy? (She sat bolt upright; she immediately marched to the phone to call the restaurant owner.)

Choose a student to read aloud Jimmy's response to Granny on page 79 when he gets her message. Ask the students what other ways Jimmy could have responded. Point out that his response—apologizing—was the right one.

▶ [interpretive] What does Hiram mean when he says that Jimmy "wakes you up"? (that Jimmy makes people think about the things around them in nature, the things only children would notice)

[literal] What does Jimmy find that he wants his family to listen to? (a conch shell)

[interpretive] What does Paul mean by the phrase "The dog isn't with Jimmy. Jimmy is with the dog"? (Blackie was leading; Jimmy was following.)

[literal] Whose voice is heard saying "Hey, kid!"? (the man who took Blackie)

[literal] What is Granny's immediate response? (She says she will call the police.)

Choose a student to read aloud the last three paragraphs on page 83 that tell how Granny and Hiram respond.

Scriptural Application

Ask the students to think about how they usually respond when they are corrected for their behavior by an adult. Read Proverbs 19:20. Ask them how they think the Lord wants them to respond. (to receive it, to obey it, to be willing to change) Ask them what He promises if they obey. (wisdom)

Pausing to Rest

Tell the students that they will have to wait to find out what happens to Jimmy and Blackie. Direct them to mark their places in their books.

Going Further

Journey into Heritage Studies—Maps

Tell the students to take out their maps of Pelican Cove (see Reproducible—Lesson 4). Put the students in groups of two and instruct them to read through Chapter 9 again, adding features to their map such as Talmadge Duncan's plot, the tide pools, and the restaurant. Instruct them to track Jimmy's path along the beach with their pencil as closely as they can from the clues he gives in the story.

Journey into Language— Writing

"Has Anyone Seen This Dog?" (Reproducible—Lesson 9)

Journey into Science

Tell the students that the scientific study of shells is called *conchology*. Provide books and articles on types of shells and how they are formed. Allow students to bring their own shells and analyze them using the resource materials.

Lesson 10

Objectives

The student will

- Understand and appreciate details of setting.
- Use context clues to comprehend the meanings of new words.
- Apply the scriptural principle of helping others.
- Identify with story characters.

Planning the Trip

Gather

❏ A toy Ferris wheel or a picture of a Ferris wheel.

❏ A Bible.

Prepare

❏ A copy of Reproducible—Lesson 10A for each student.

❏ Slips of paper and bowls for use with Reproducible—Lesson 10B.

❏ A list of the following sentences on the chalkboard:

When the child lost his mother, he began to run <u>frantically</u> up and down each aisle.

Mother laid the <u>protesting</u> baby, kicking and screaming, in her crib.

His clothes were <u>rumpled</u>, as though he had slept in them.

Because the machinery had some <u>kinks</u>, the toy train would not run properly.

I have a <u>suspicion</u> that this money is fake.

Packing Up

Introducing the Story

Show the students the toy or miniature Ferris wheel you have brought. Ask the following questions.

► Have you ever ridden a Ferris wheel? If so, when and where?

► What did you think of the experience?

Explain that Ferris wheels were called *pleasure wheels* at first. They were renamed after George Ferris, an engineer, who designed the world's largest wheel in 1893. Ferris's wheel did not have seats but closed-in cabs that could hold 60 passengers each. About 2,160 people could ride Ferris's wheel at one time.

Tell the students that a Ferris wheel will play an important part in the chapter they will read for today.

Developing Word Meaning

Read the sentences from the chalkboard. After each sentence, allow the students to guess the meaning of the underlined word from its context. (*frantically—characterized by rapid, nervous activity; protesting—objecting to; rumpled—wrinkled; kinks—difficulties or flaws; suspicion—suspecting wrong with little proof or evidence*) Allow the students to act out the first three words.

Traveling Along

Setting the Purpose

Encourage the students to notice all the details about the amusement park that the author works into the story in this chapter.

Reading and Thinking

Direct the students to read silently pages 85-94. Ask the following questions.

► *[literal]* Where does Blackie run after Bill grabs for him? (*toward the amusement park*)

[critical] Why is it harder for Jimmy to dodge the crowds than Blackie? (*Possible answer: Dogs are smaller, quicker, and better at dodging than people are.*)

[interpretive] How can you tell that the attendant at the fair is angry? (*He calls them "crazy," and he thrashes at Blackie with a broom.*)

Choose a student to read aloud what the attendant says to Jimmy and Blackie on page 86.

► *[literal]* How does Jimmy pick up Blackie's trail again after he has been in the duck pond? (*He follows the wet tracks Blackie has left behind.*)

[critical] How is the Ferris-wheel operator different from the ring-toss-booth attendant? (*Possible answer: He is friendlier, more helpful.*)

[interpretive] How does the Ferris-wheel operator help Jimmy and Blackie escape from Bill? (*He sends Bill all the way to the top after Jimmy and Blackie jump out.*)

[appreciative] How do you feel after Bill has been sent to the top of the Ferris wheel?

Choose two students to read aloud the conversation on page 90 between the Ferris-wheel operator and Jimmy after Jimmy jumps out.

▶ *[literal]* What stop does Blackie make before heading away from the amusement park? *(He stops at the ice-cream booth.)*

[interpretive] What discovery does Jimmy make about Blackie at the ice-cream booth? *(that Blackie likes ice cream)*

[interpretive] At what point in the chapter does Jimmy make his most important discovery? *(at the very end)*

[literal] What is this discovery? *(The nut the squirrel wants looks just like the clay ball containing the jewel that Blackie found before.)*

[critical] Why do you think the author waited until the very end of the chapter to have Jimmy make this discovery? *(Accept all answers, but lead the students to see that the author was trying to make the reader want to read on to the next chapter right away instead of stopping.)*

[appreciative] How do you feel at the end of the chapter?

Choose a student to read the last paragraph of the chapter on page 94 where Jimmy makes his important discovery.

Scriptural Application

Ask the students to name some ways people are helpful to Jimmy in this chapter. *(The Ferris-wheel operator holds Bill at the top so that Jimmy can escape; the ice-cream lady shares a cone with him and Blackie.)* Read Philippians 2:3-4. Ask the students to name ways they could look "on the things of others" in their homes and at school.

Pausing to Rest

Tell the students that they will have to read the final chapter to find out whether Jimmy's suspicion is correct. Direct them to mark their places in their books.

Going Further

Journey into Game Fun
"Through the Park"
(Reproducible—Lesson 10A)

Journey into Story Elements—Setting
"Ready, Get Set"
(Reproducible—Lesson 10B)

Lesson 11

Objectives

The student will

- Identify with the characters' search for treasure.

- Use textual clues to comprehend the meanings of new words.

- Apply the scriptural principle of replacing covetousness with right desires.

- Understand the figurative language in *The Treasure of Pelican Cove.*

Planning the Trip

Gather

- ❏ Clay or play dough.
- ❏ Several jellybeans.
- ❏ A Bible.

Prepare

- ❏ A copy of Reproducible—Lesson 11A for each student.
- ❏ Copies of Reproducible—Lesson 11B and 11D for students, as needed.
- ❏ A copy of Reproducible—Lesson 11E for each student.
- ❏ A list of the following words on the chalkboard:
  - intent
  - surged
  - hovered
  - swagger
  - minor

Packing Up

Introducing the Story

Wrap each jellybean in clay. Direct a game of "Hide the Clay Ball" with the students. Choose one student to leave the room while you hide a clay-wrapped jellybean in view of the remaining students. When the student outside returns, instruct the other students to give him clues by telling him he is "hot" (close) or "cold" (distant) in relation to the jellybean. After he finds the bean, allow him to keep it and to hide another while a different student waits outside. Repeat the game as many times as desired.

Developing Word Meaning

Read the words on the chalkboard aloud and give the students the following clues.

One of the words means "a person who is not yet a legal adult." It also means something small or a certain kind of key in music. It is the opposite of major. *(minor)*

One of the words means "concentrating; being very attentive." It can also mean "an aim or a purpose." It sounds like a place you would sleep when camping. *(intent)*

One of the words means "to walk proudly; to strut." It has some of the same sounds in it that the word *brag* does. *(swagger)* After the students have guessed this word, allow one of them to act it out.

One of the words means "rushed forward like waves." The word sounds a little like the sound the sea makes when it rushes to the shore. *(surged)*

Onc of thc words mcans "staycd ncar." It can also mean "remained floating or fluttering over." It is often used when referring to birds, butterflies, and helicopters. *(hovered)*

Ask the students to use each word in a sentence.

Traveling Along

Setting the Purpose

Tell the students that the family makes an important decision at the end of this chapter. Encourage them to watch for this decision as they read.

Reading and Thinking

Direct the students to read silently pages 95-104. Ask the following questions.

▶ *[interpretive]* What does Jimmy mean when he yells, "This is it!"? *(They have found Pegleg's treasure.)*

[interpretive] What clue lets Jimmy know he has found Pegleg's treasure? *(an iron hinge from the treasure chest)*

Choose a student to read the paragraph that describes Jimmy's finding the clay ball on page 95.

▶ *[interpretive]* What is Bill's attitude toward Jimmy when he discovers him? *(He says he doesn't need him anymore; he tells him to get away from the treasure.)*

[literal] What clues let Jimmy know that help is on its way? *(He hears sirens, and he sees people running toward him.)*

Choose two students to read aloud the conversation between Bill and Jimmy in the middle of page 96.

▶ *[interpretive]* How do you think Jimmy feels when he sees Granny and Hiram again? *(happy, excited, relieved, not scared anymore)*

[interpretive] To whom does Jimmy say, "Take good care of Pegleg's treasure"? *(the squirrels)*

[literal] What bothers Jimmy about the way Elizabeth Anne welcomes him home? *(She kisses him and mothers him too much.)*

[appreciative] Do you have an older sister who likes to mother you? Why do you think she treats you this way?

[interpretive] What does the author mean when she says Jimmy "had developed a swagger"? *(He was proud.)*

Choose a student to read aloud the paragraph at the bottom of page 99 that tells why Jimmy was proud.

▶ *[literal]* What kind of jewel does Granny find under the clay? *(a pigeon ruby)*

[literal] What is a pigeon ruby? *(a big ruby worth a lot of money)*

[literal] What does Granny say the children's parents will do with the money? *(put it in a college fund)*

Choose a student to read aloud the paragraph on page 100 that tells what Granny plans to do with the ruby.

▶ *[literal]* How does Jimmy behave while the others are discussing where the rest of the treasure might be? *(He fidgets, opens his mouth, and shuts it again.)*

[interpretive] What do Jimmy's actions tell you? *(He is struggling with the decision of whether to tell his family what he knows about the treasure.)*

[literal] What does he finally decide? *(He tells his family the squirrels have the treasure.)*

[literal] What does Paul want to do? *(go get the jewels from the squirrels)*

[appreciative] What would you want to do?

Choose a student to read aloud the paragraph that begins at the bottom of page 102 in which Jimmy gives his reason for not wanting to tell anyone about the treasure.

▶ *[interpretive]* What does Jimmy mean when he says, "People act funny when they are hunting treasure"? *(People stop acting like themselves; they become so interested in the treasure that they are willing to hurt others to get what they want.)*

[interpretive] What does Paul mean when he says, "The fun was in the chase"? *(It was more exciting to look for the treasure than to actually find it.)*

[critical] Do you think the family made the right decision not to tell where the treasure was? *(Accept any answer.)*

Choose a student to read what the children and Hiram said on page 104 as they did their four-hand shake.

Scriptural Application
Read I Timothy 6:10-11 to the students. Ask the students what the verse says is the root of all evil. *(the love of money)* Ask them what we are to follow after instead. *(righteousness, godliness, faith, love, patience, and meekness)* Make a list on the chalkboard of their suggestions of things on which Christians should focus.

Pausing to Rest

Tell the students to close their books. Invite them to tell what their favorite part was in *The Treasure of Pelican Cove.*

Going Further

Journey into Thinking Skills— Critical Thinking
"Think About It"
(Reproducible—Lesson 11A)

Journey into Language— Speaking
Have the students do character speeches using Reproducibles—Lesson 11B and 11D. Note the Teacher's Guide for this activity, Reproducible—Lesson 11C.

Journey into the Story
Extend the enjoyment of reading *The Treasure of Pelican Cove* with a "Beach Day." (See suggestions on the folder and Sample Letter to Parents, Reproducible— Lesson 11E.)

Who Is It?

▶ Fill in the blanks with the correct letter.
   Some answers will be used more than once.

A. Jimmy	C. Paul	E. Hiram
B. Granny	D. Elizabeth Anne	F. Blackie

1. Gets embarrassed by her brother _____

2. Uses force to make Jimmy behave _____

3. Likes dogs _____

4. Owns Land's End _____

5. Eats bones _____

6. Likes to tease Granny _____

7. Does not like tourist traps _____

8. Likes the large bedroom _____

9. Doesn't mind sharing a room with Jimmy _____

The Treasure of Pelican Cove, Reproducible—Lesson 1A

See last page for answer key.

© 1998 BJU Press. Limited license to copy granted on copyright page.

What's to See at the Sea?

sea bass
sea horse
sea oats   sea lion
sea dog   sea fan
sea lettuce
sea grape

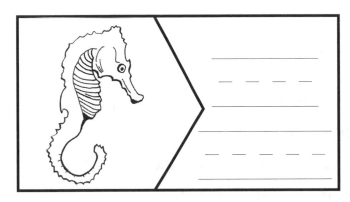

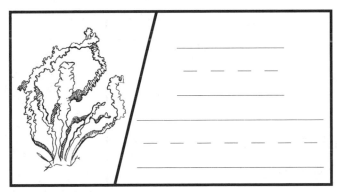

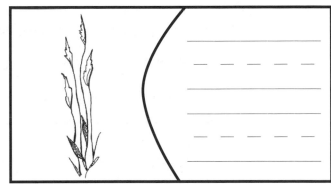

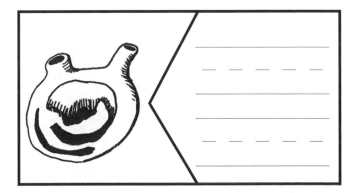

The Treasure of Pelican Cove, Reproducible—Lesson 1B

See last page for answer key.

© 1998 BJU Press. Limited license to copy granted on copyright page.

Teacher's Guide for Reproducible—Lesson 1B

1. Direct the students to choose a word from the word list and write it on the correct puzzle piece. They may color the illustrations if they wish.

2. Check the answers together as a group, allowing students to correct any errors.

3. Ask the students to carefully cut apart the puzzle pieces and place them in the envelope.

4. Suggest that the students give the puzzle envelope to a younger relative or friend and ask him to try matching the pieces.

© 1998 BJU Press. Limited license to copy granted on copyright page.

X or O?

▶ Write an **O** in front of each true statement and an **X** in front of each false statement.

_____ 1. Blackie and Jimmy are glad to see each other.

_____ 2. Hiram tells Jimmy the story of Old Black Jack.

_____ 3. Jimmy and Granny find everything peaceful and calm on the widow's walk.

_____ 4. Jimmy's mother thinks her children learn character at Granny's.

_____ 5. Jimmy wants to find a big shell like Hiram's washed up on the beach.

_____ 6. Hiram is glad that Jimmy hasn't changed.

_____ 7. The storm is not a real hurricane.

_____ 8. Blackie likes to chase rabbits at the amusement park.

_____ 9. Jimmy stays up late to watch the storm.

_____ 10. As soon as Blackie brings Jimmy the clay ball, he knows there is a jewel inside.

© 1998 BJU Press. Limited license to copy granted on copyright page.

See last page for answer key.

Sea Shapes

A Chest of Missing Words

▶ Fill in each blank with a word from the treasure chest below.

1. The jewel Jimmy has found is an _____.

2. Granny calls Hiram's tall tales _____ stories.

3. The hero in Hiram's story is his _____.

4. The first unusual thing Granddad noticed

   was a _____.

5. Inside the boat was a

   _____.

6. Granddad knew the pirate had a peg leg by

   his _____ in the sand.

7. Hiram thinks Pegleg's treasure is hidden somewhere _____.

Whose Tracks?

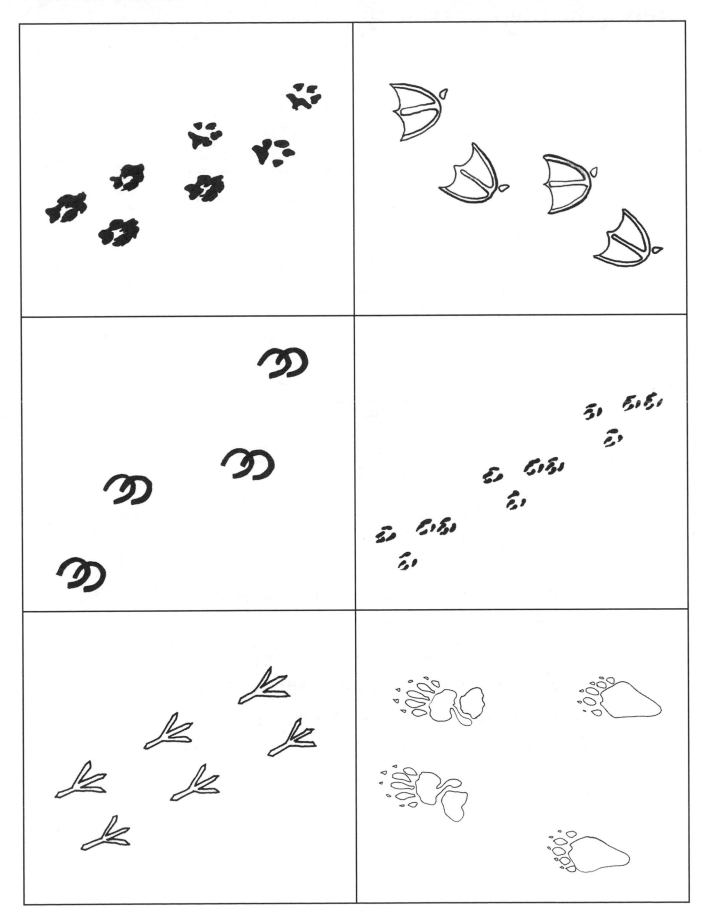

Teacher's Guide for Reproducible—Lesson 3B

Enlarge Reproducible—3B so that each set of tracks is large enough to be seen by all members of the group. Cut the sets of tracks apart and write the corresponding animal's name on the back of each card.

1. dog
2. duck
3. horse
4. rabbit
5. bird
6. bear

Direct a student to choose a card and show the front side (with the tracks) to the group, but not the name on the back. The student should make appropriate noises or actions until someone guesses what animal made the tracks.

X Marks the Spot

▶ Where did Blackie find the jewel? Imagine and draw the path that he might have taken around Pelican Cove, and place an **X** where you think the treasure might be buried.

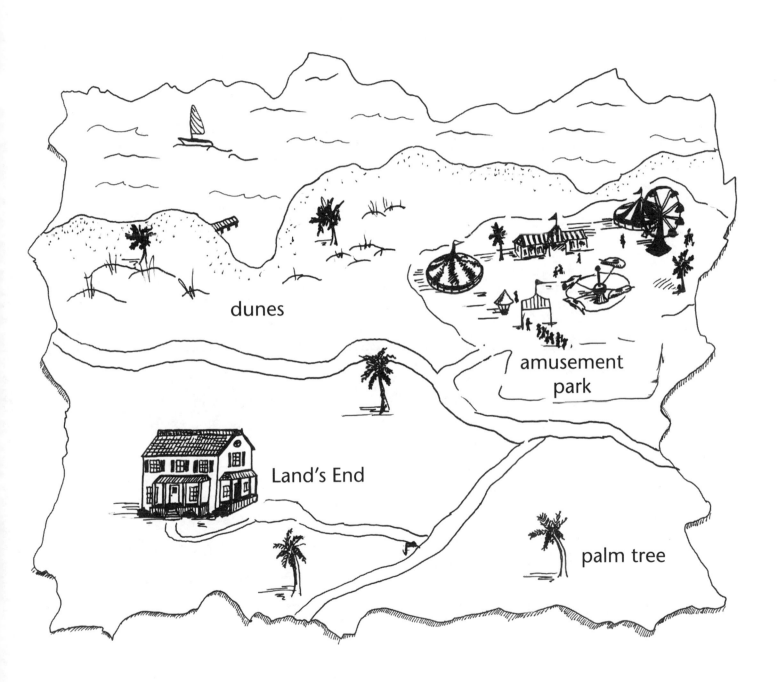

dunes

amusement park

Land's End

palm tree

Filling in the Holes

▶ Choose the best answer to complete each sentence.
  Write the answer in the blank.

1. Granny has been to see _____.

   the mayor   the museum curator   the librarian

2. Hiram thinks Mr. Culpepper is _____.

   friendly   shy   nosy

3. The first thing Jimmy sees from the window the

   next morning is _____.

   holes   Blackie   people

4. Hiram is angry with _____.

   Jake   the mayor   Miss Abbott

5. The mayor does not _____

   _____.

   call a town meeting   reward Jimmy   close the beach

6. Miss Abbott is the town's _____.

   curator   mayor   librarian

What If?

▶ Think about the Sea Scene you made. Write a story about something in the scene or about something that might happen there. Then roll up your story and put it in the can for someone else to read.

Arranging Shells

▶ Put the events in each group in story order.

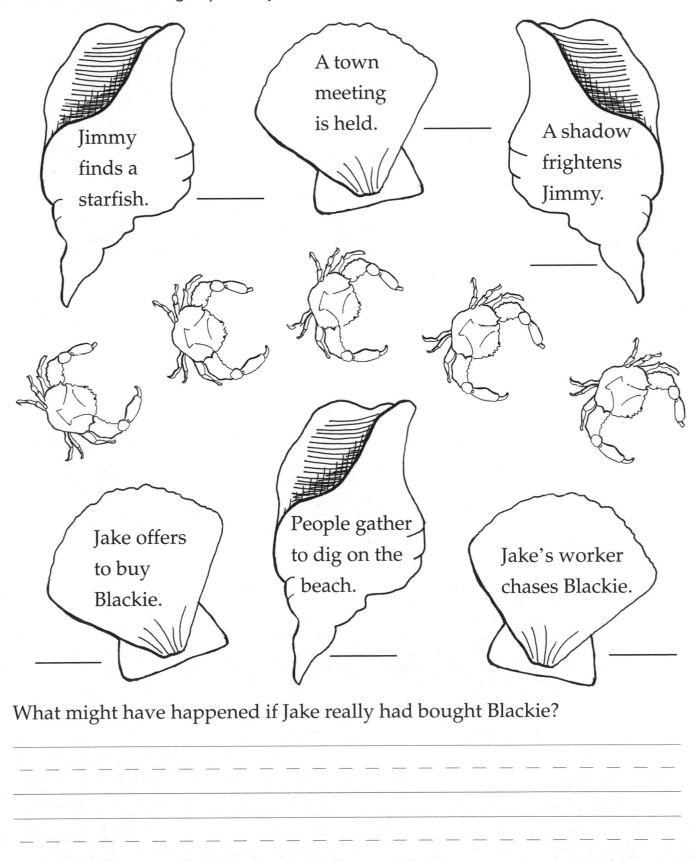

Jimmy finds a starfish. ____

A town meeting is held. ____

A shadow frightens Jimmy. ____

Jake offers to buy Blackie. ____

People gather to dig on the beach. ____

Jake's worker chases Blackie. ____

What might have happened if Jake really had bought Blackie?

_____

_____

_____

_____

See last page for answer key.

Where Has My Little Dog Gone?

Septimus Winner

German Folksong

Oh where, oh where has my lit-tle dog gone? Oh where, oh where can he be?_____ With his tail cut short and his ears cut long, Oh where, oh where can he be?_____

"Where Has My Little Dog Gone?" arrangement, © 1987 BJU Press. All rights reserved.

On the Right Track

▶ Jimmy saw boot tracks in the sand with paw prints alongside, and then he followed them to where the paw prints ended. He knew that someone had taken Blackie. Choose one set of tracks below and tell what you think might have happened. What if you saw these tracks in the sand?

Dog and bird tracks

Boy and rabbit tracks

Man and horse tracks

The "Jake" Mistake

▶ Jake has turned out to be a different kind of person from what Jimmy expected. Color the shells that tell something true about Jake.

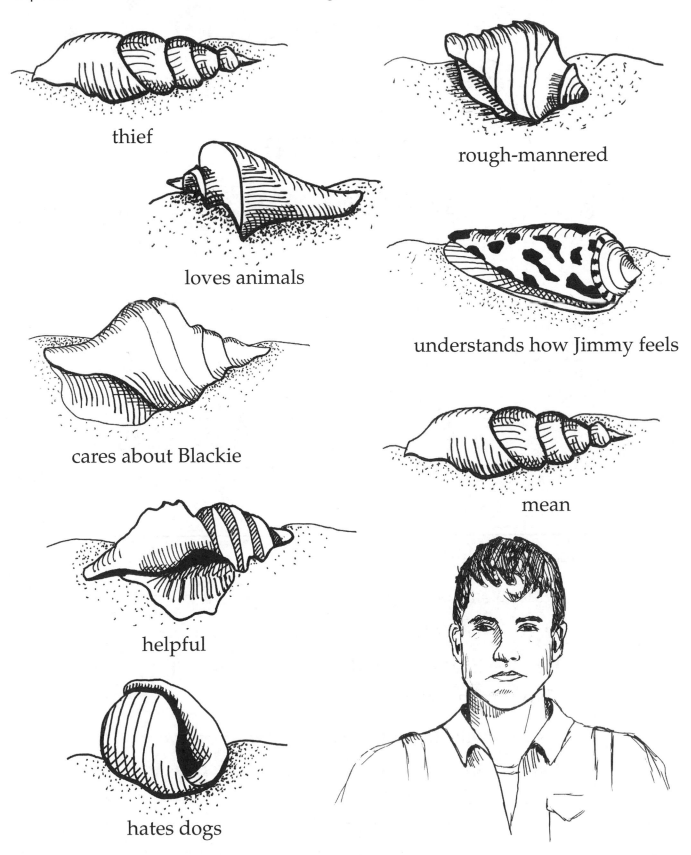

thief

rough-mannered

loves animals

understands how Jimmy feels

cares about Blackie

mean

helpful

hates dogs

How Come?

Blackie
is missing.

Blackie brings
a jewel
to Jimmy.

Jimmy tries to
follow Blackie.

Granny talks to
Mr. Culpepper.

Jake offers to
buy Blackie.

People dig holes
in the beach.

A workman sees
Blackie explore
the holes.

Teacher's Guide

1. Draw a similar diagram on a transparency
   or on the chalkboard.

2. Write a situation from the story, such as that
   above, in the oval.

3. Ask students to suggest some of the story events
   that led up to this situation. An advanced group
   could list the events in order.

Has Anyone Seen This Dog?

▶ If someone asked Jimmy to describe Blackie, what would he say? Circle the words that best tell about Blackie.

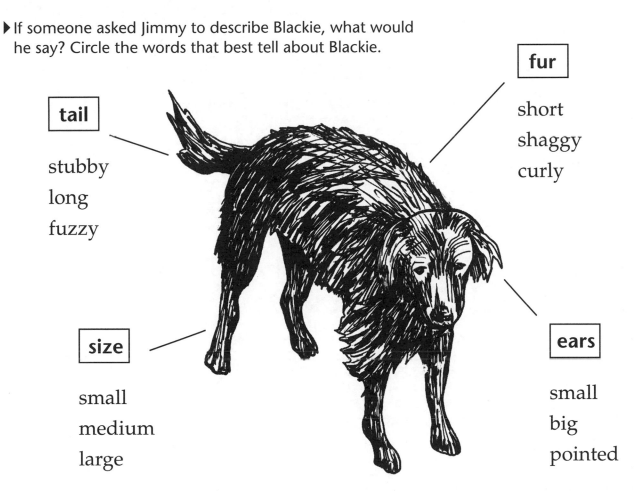

fur

short
shaggy
curly

tail

stubby
long
fuzzy

size

small
medium
large

ears

small
big
pointed

▶ Pretend that your dog is lost. You want to put a notice in the newspaper. Use the words above to tell about him.

★ LOST! ★

My dog has _____ fur and _____ ears.

His tail is _____. He is a _____-sized

dog. His name is _____.

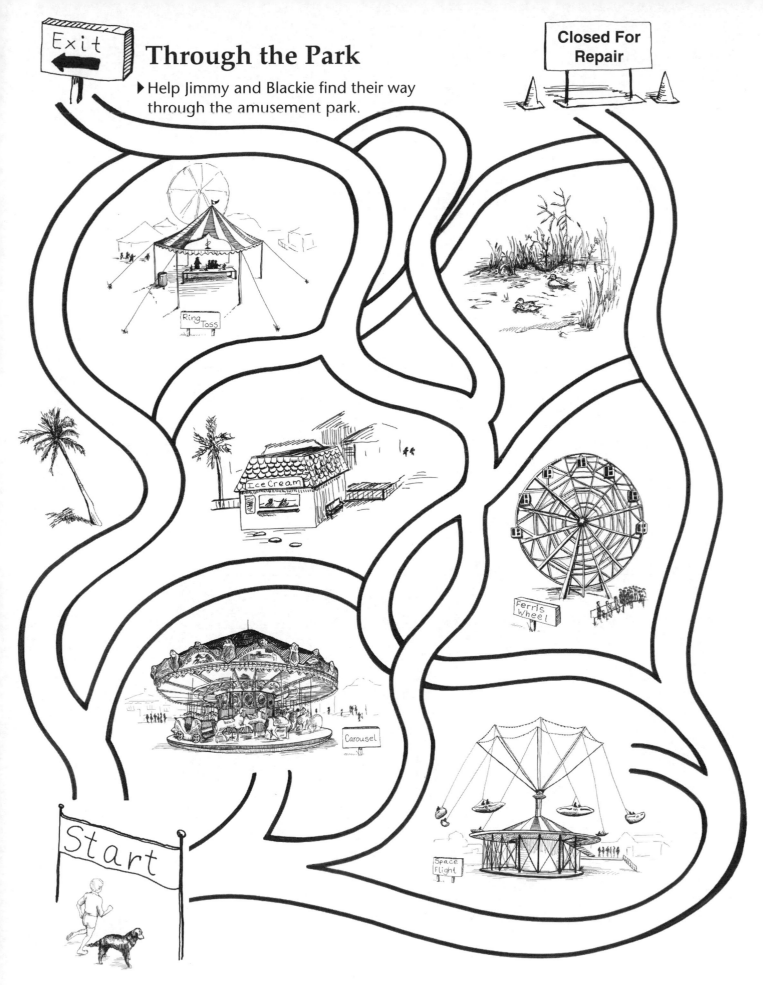

Through the Park

▶ Help Jimmy and Blackie find their way through the amusement park.

Exit

Closed For Repair

Ring Toss

Ice Cream

Ferris Wheel

Carousel

Space Flight

Start

The Treasure of Pelican Cove, Reproducible—Lesson 10A

Ready, Get Set

▶ Explain to the students that **setting** is a literary term meaning the surroundings in which a story takes place. Setting includes the place, time, and circumstances during which the events of a story unfold. Discuss with the students what the setting of *The Treasure of Pelican Cove* is.

Divide the students into four small groups for this exercise.

Write the following elements of setting on separate slips of paper:

- a jungle
- a grocery store
- a zoo
- a castle

- midnight
- early morning
- noon
- evening

- winter
- summer
- spring
- fall

Put the slips into three different bowls and have each group draw a slip from each bowl. Tell them that the three slips they have drawn make up the setting for their story. Give them time in class to use their new setting and write a short retelling of Jimmy and Blackie's chase through the amusement park. Encourage them to include specific details that will show which elements of setting they are using. Choose one person in each group to read the finished story to the class.

Think About It

▶ Draw a line to the picture that best tells what was meant by the statement.

1.

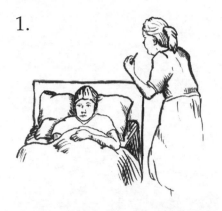

"You've got treasure-hunting fever."

2.

3.

"This truck of Hiram's could find its own way home on a dark night!"

4.

5.

"Just don't you forget that Blackie is no spring chicken."

6.

7.

"Has the look of my Jake when things don't go his way."

8.

See last page for answer key.

Granny's Speech

▶ This is what Granny might have said. Use the
words in the box below to fill in the blanks.

police	Bill	Blackie	Mrs. Lester	Jake
squirrels	Pelican Cove	Mr. Culpepper	receiver	

Hello, my name is Granny. I live in _____.

My dog's name is _____. When Jimmy found a jewel on

the beach, I showed it to _____.
After Blackie disappeared, I took the children to

_____ 's home. I thought she would know where

we could find Blackie. She didn't know, but her son, _____,

took us to see _____. I could tell that Bill was up to
no good. We took Blackie home and attached a special

kind of bug to his collar. Then we listened over the _____
as Blackie and Jimmy explored the island. When I heard

Bill's voice, I called the _____. They took care of Bill!

Jimmy was safe, and the _____ kept the treasure.

See last page for answer key.

Teacher's Guide for
Reproducibles—Lesson 11B and 11D

Character Speeches

Give each student the option of doing his character speech as either Jimmy or Granny. When the students have made their choices, give a copy of the appropriate speech to each one (Reproducibles—Lesson 11B and 11D). Allow the students time to fill in the blanks in their character's speech, using the word bank at the top of the page.

Assign each student a time to perform his speech. He may either read it or present it from memory. Encourage the students to make their speeches as "real" as possible, using vocal and facial expression and dressing like the character they are representing.

Jimmy's Speech

▶ This is what Jimmy might have said. Use the words from the box to fill in the blanks.

jewel	squirrels	Jake
Blackie	bug	receiver
grandson	Bill	Old Pegleg

Hi, my name is Jimmy. I am Granny's _____. Gran

has a dog named _____. While I played with Blackie

on the beach, I discovered a _____ in a ball of clay.

Hiram said the jewel might be part of _____'s
treasure. Granny let us search the beach, but we ran into a problem.

Someone stole Blackie. I thought _____ took Blackie.
We found Blackie at Bill's home. After we went home, Granny attached a

_____ to my pocket. This allowed Hiram and the
others to listen to Blackie and me as we explored the island.

_____ followed Blackie and me around the island.

Granny heard his voice on the _____
and called the police. After I found the treasure,
I decided it would be best to leave it for the

_____.

The Treasure of Pelican Cove, Reproducible—Lesson 11D

See last page for answer key.

Sample Letter to Parents

Dear parents:

For several weeks we have been linking literature to many other classroom activities as we read *The Treasure of Pelican Cove* by Milly Howard. We will be celebrating our completion of the book and extending our enjoyment of the story with "A Day at the Beach" on _____ . We will have food, stories, songs, and games with a beach theme. You may help to make this day memorable for your child by making sure that he or she brings the following:

- A beach towel

- A small treasure sealed into a paper lunch bag. Prepare the child to give three clues about the treasure.

- Sunglasses and/or sun hat are optional. All items should be labeled with the child's name.

If you would like to help provide refreshments for our special day, please return the slip below by _____ .

Thank you for your involvement in our learning and fun.

_____

- -

Yes! I would like to help provide refreshments for "A Day at the Beach." Please contact me.

Home phone number _____   Best time to call _____

Business phone number _____   Best time to call _____

Student's name _____

Parent's signature _____

Please return this slip to school by _____ .

The Treasure of Pelican Cove, Reproducible—Lesson 11E